Yellow Torchlight and the Blues

by **Emma Lee**

original plus

this collection, 'Yellow Torchlight and the Blues',
first published in Britain by
'original plus'
Flat 3
18 Oxford Grove
Ilfracombe
Devon EX34 9HQ

ISBN 0953359190

printed and bound by
The Pembrokeshire Press, Print House, Parc y Shwt, High Street,
Fishguard, Pembrokeshire. SA65 9AP
(01348 873979)

Emma Lee - Author Profile

Emma Lee was born in South Gloucestershire and settled in Leicester where she now lives with her husband, Paul, and young daughter. Although she'd met Gold Medalist Robin Cousins and the then youngest pair skaters to represent Britain at the Winter Olympics, Emma's own figure skating career - destined for the chorus line of Holiday on Ice - was cut short by a knee injury. So she took up hanging around bars and clubs reviewing bands and meeting liggers and hangers-on. Managed to squeeze in some foreign travel: seeing the Berlin Wall before it fell, Moscow and St Petersburg when Russia was the Union of Soviet Socialist Republics as well as visiting Ireland, Germany, Czech Republic and France. More recently she swapped the chill of clubs and bars' beer-sticky floors for the relative comforts of cinemas, when time around family, writing and job commitments permits. She currently works as an Information Assistant. Previously she's worked as secretary, personnel assistant and for MENCAP.

Emma's poems have been nominated for the Forward Best Poem Prize, broadcast on BBC Radio, prize-winners in competitions and widely published in anthologies, magazines and webzines. She was commissioned for the Newarke and Sherwood Millennium Poetry Project and has performed her work, most notably at Leicester City Football Club and Leicester's Guildhall. Her short stories are also widely published and one, "Restoration" was runner-up in Writing Magazine's Annual Ghost Story Competition. Emma writes regular reviews for 10th Muse, The Journal, Poetry Quarterly Review and New Hope International and ad hoc reviews for other publications. She's a member of Leicester Writers' Club and Leicester Poetry Society and adjudicated Nottingham Writers' Club's 70th anniversary prose competition.

acknowledgements
some of these poems have appeared in the following publications:

Aabye; Borderlines; Envoi; Erased, Sigh, Sigh (US); "Exit 21" (Leicester Poetry Society edited by Ian McMillan)*; Fabric; Fire; The Frogmore Papers; The Interpreter's House; Iota; The Journal; The Journal of Contemporary Anglo Scandinavian Poetry; "Let's Shout about It"* (QQ Press, edited Alan J Carter); *"Listening to the Birth of Crystals"* (Paula Brown Press, edited Alan Corkish and Andrew Taylor); *Obsessed with Pipework; Other Poetry; Poetry Monthly; Poetry Nottingham International; Rain Dog; Roadworks; Sepia; Smiths Knoll; Spume; Staple; 10th Muse; "Target Babes (best of Target magazine)"* Forty Winks Press, edited Bryn Fortey;

"Andrew" was runner-up in the Headway Poetry Competition;
"Autumn Colours" won Third Prize in the LOROS (Leicestershire Organisation for the Relief of Suffering) *Poetry Competition*
"Even amidst the fierce flames the golden lotus can be planted" Highly Commended in Leicester Poetry Society's Open Poetry Competition 2003, also displayed in Loughborough Library as part of the National Poetry Day celebrations 2003
"Julie" was published by Leicester City Libraries as a bookmark for National Poetry Day 2002
"Sunlight: North Dublin" was awarded a Diploma in the Scottish International Poetry Competition 2003

for Paul and Miranda

contents

contents continued

Preview

The author fidgets into a chair
crosses his legs
cleans out a piece of fingernail dirt
folds his arms, nods.

The special effects technician
starts the ten minute excerpt,
reminds himself to breathe.
The author watches,
his mouth makes chewing motions,
fingers tap a beat
that isn't in time with the score.

"How is this possible?"
asks the author.

The technician's heartbeat
feels as loud as the movie's soundtrack.
He grips the chair arm.
He sees the miniature models
stuffed with lit fibre optic wires,
shot in a blacked out room
to create a dense futurescape.

"It's how I saw it
when I wrote the book."

The technician breathes out,
says nothing.

Blotched Notes

I am your secrets:

your sister notched another A+,
your brother set off the fire alarms again.
Because a teacher stripped your confidence
your friend coached you in maths.
You envied her ice-skater's figure:
your ribs didn't show in the bathroom mirror.

I recorded calorific values:
this week soup and water only.
You took me to the library
to avoid family dinners.

Weekends we visited your father
- a rapid of shops, treats and presents.
He disapproved of your contacts
with a flighty half-sister
who dreamt of red sports cars
and freeways with no destinations.

This time I recorded sticky buns,
doughnuts, choux pastries, cream horns,
cakes, turnovers, bars of chocolate
and a smudge of vomit.

I helped your GP's diagnosis.
Soon you stopped scribbling your thoughts
in blotched biro on my pages.
You also stopped speaking to your friend:
the one who bought me for you.

Mark

As the fire alarm rang we filed out, welcomed
the break. Year Six teachers counted heads
but no one called the fire brigade.

I look out. You stand apart
hunched near a separate class line.
Your watery eyes stare at the word *start*
chalked on the ground. Later you'll wait for your stepfather.
You'll play with toys that once belonged to others
while your mother fixes a door latch with twine
and feeds the caged birds in that house of odours.
five doors down from ours.

I want to say it's OK to be a slow reader,
that there's no crime in being
average. Remind you of shared cigarettes
where, for all my mother-encouraged reading,
you were better than me at inventing stories
that you could raise beyond dreams
as if you really believed in them.
And somehow find a talent for your light fingers.

Andrew

When you fell over
there were no tears, but a shriek
from untuned vocal chords.
I kept talking to your silence,
washed and put a plaster on your cut knee.
You zoomed back to climb inside a fort
blockading yourself behind a high wall.

"He's affectionate, really.
Intelligent for a five-year-old."
Your mother held your hand as she spoke.
Behind her back, the playscheme leader shook his head.
A sudden pull
and you sprinted towards me.

After that I got used to a tug on my arm,
a directional pointer.
The palm-slap on table top
that meant agitation.
A hug for reward.

You learnt "Yes,", "Let me finish this first,"
"No, it's lunch time,"
where you'd show me
the food your mother had packed
before bolting it down and running back
to the people-empty, toy-filled hall.

Some Empty Seats are taken

You remember don't you..?
his arthritic finger knocks against the bus window
although he's looking at the seat next to him.
His worn tweed cap almost covers
what's left of his thin grey hair.

... You remember that time..?
His faded green anorak is zipped closed.
Red jeans cling to the contours of his knees.
His feet in nearly-new Reeboks
twitch to a rhythm of some old song.

.... when we walked..?
His tone is anxious, as if on a first date.
His wedding band catches sunlight.
He turns to look straight ahead
as the bus reaches the city centre.

He waits for the other passengers to alight.
Then pulls himself up and bites his lip
as he leaves without looking
at the empty seat he'd sat next to.

Known as Crow

For him, time is a set of numbers:
a vector with magnitude
but no direction.

At 4 am the TV was smashed through bedsit windows:
"To shut it up, to stop the walls closing in.
I wanted to feel the air, feel alive."
Boarded up, re-glazed, re-smashed.

Housing benefit? "It's the landlord's
but it's the only money I get.
I think I'm supposed to sign on,"
he shrugs his watchless arms.

Evicted, Crow says he prefers the streets,
"Nothing closes me in out here.
And people help with food.
My friend lets me wash."

His wide disorientating eyes
look out from under dreads.
A grimy parka covers a baggy jumper
over tough blue jeans and his hiking boots
that are always striding somewhere.

Final Score

You put forward your list of excuses -
can't stand hospitals
can't bear seeing my wife in pain
she'll be better off without me -
and escaped to watch your team draw nil nil.

Which was more agonizing -
the football match?
picturing your wife in labour?
or her final revenge:
calling the baby after a rival football team?

So you buy roses, red naturally,
as you visit the baby daughter
you'd have named Charlotte Georgina.
Or Charlie George
as she sat on your knee on the terraces.

But now you have to take Chelsea to Highbury
and hope to win.

Highbury Tannoy announcement
"Your wife has just given birth. You are at Arsenal versus Spurs
To make matters worse, she's just called it Chelsea.

Little Wall

"*Do not fear for the child / its gold is hid*"
(Jorie Graham, "Motive Elusive")

"Daddy," he said under his breath,
naming the voice he heard
as the door slammed.

"White," he stroked a bar on his cot.
He liked naming things:
it made Mommy smile.

"White," was the wall too,
Then his Mommy made a sound
he knew how to make:

he put his hand over his mouth,
clamped it tight
and tried to say "Mommy."

He pulled himself up
so he could touch the wall.
"Window," his fingers traced

the borders of shadow
following the outline of a pane.
There were more sounds

like the one he knew how to make.
He touched his cot bar,
that felt smooth and slightly warm.

But the wall felt different:
like Mommy's skin when she was cold.
"Wall," he almost sat

when it shook with a thud
like the one he heard
when he fell and hit his head.

A few white flakes drifted down.
He caught one.
"Little wall," he looked again.

A door slammed, "Daddy gone."
"Sssh," there was no sound
not even the one Mommy

made when she slept.
He dropped the paint-flake
and stretched his hands

to the wall, thumbs touching,
either side of the shadow.
It looked like... like Mommy's picture

He named it, "Butterfly."

Dad, Not Daddy

I woke up frightened
because dark means sleep
and the lounge window got broken.

He's not Daddy anymore
and last night he was here.
My sister's Dad was in the kitchen.

There was a car
and its blue light wasn't working.
Then there was a loud noise,
then quiet.
No... there was crying.
Not Daddy was crying,
and Mummy shut the door.

Dad makes breakfast.
He doesn't smell of beer.
And lets me put the light on
if I want to.

The Room of Dolls

A thousand blue eyes stare
from perfect creamy faces
with expressionless, closed mouths.
Each in a pretty, lace-edged dress
and buckled shoes with white socks.
Each fixed at the age of five.

The same age as a girl
who had a novel's character
based on her: a vampire
who was forever five years old.

A teacher's slip meant a boy
discovered he'd had a sister
who'd died of leukaemia.
He enters his mother's private room,
redolent with magnolias.
He sees a thousand staring eyes.

The Clever Daughter

"Given and yet not given
clothed and unclothed
neither walking nor riding":
solve the riddle
and the feudal lord would freeze taxes.

But first there was work to do:
nets had to be mended
animals be fed
meals cooked
house swept.

Let the villagers watch and wait.

I wanted a little piece of fame:
to be a carving somewhere
that people would admire
then puzzle over
as the story was forgotten.

I could see that carving -
in solid oak
the detail done with care
yet strong enough
to last centuries -

as I caught a live hare,
wrapped myself in fishing nets,
swung my leg over my goat's back
and hopped along the path.

Morella

I would have called you Morella,
Ella for friends and family,
promised this is the first and last poem for you,
I'd have shown you how to trace your left-handedness
back through family generations to Victoria's reign,
watched you try out your talents,
swapped gossip, homework notes, clothes,
I would've supported your choice of when to leave home,
had you been more than an egg that wouldn't anchor,

had you been more than an egg that wouldn't anchor,
I would've supported your choice of when to leave home,
swapped gossip, homework notes, clothes,
watched you try out your talents,
back through family generations to Victoria's reign
I'd have shown you how to trace your left-handedness,
promised this is the first and last poem for you.
Ella for friends and family,
I would have called you Morella.

ADA

The legitimate daughter of Lord Byron
and his Princess of Parallelograms
explained how Babbage's Analytical Engine
produced logical number patterns
and published the first computer program,
when card-fed looms wove repeated designs.

Is there a calculus of the nervous system?

Cancer took her without an answer.
But a Pentagon researcher deciphered her question:
the 1990s built neural networks
that mapped the software to guide smartbombs;
programs based on her concepts
now defined in US Military Standard 1815 - ADA.

Good Morning Midnight
(*after Jean Rhys*)

This hostel room is bare.
The remaining wallpaper,
wallflower-like, refuses to peel.

She's huddled into the chair,
knees drawn up to lessen
the impact of floorboard-gap draughts.

The bedcover remains unkindly crumpled.
The man in the night, as others before,
became loving by drink alone.

The wine in the dresser bottle: uncomfortably
blood-stained. And with more body
than in those bruise-coloured veins.

Outside the window the fountain
spurts so icy clear in the dying night.

“Like a child forming itself finger by finger in the dark”

My father told me I was love.
My mother said an accident,
grew like a bulb in her cold womb.
The grass would unload its dew on my feet
as I traced the flowers the frost made
and drew a star for my dead father.
Pinched red mouthfuls of berries
knowing sunset would bring punishment
after which I’d look to the black sky,
search for my father’s star.

I envied the magnolia,
drinking its own scent.
Eternity stretched like boredom.
I counted the pills, but not enough
to kill this thinness, light as paper.

And I became a bride. You were real,
handsomely featureless,
would waste afternoons staring at the sky.
I gave you children. Then
I drew pity from the others on the ward.
I took my ring off. It caught the sun.
I put it back on. This is my finger
touching the photo. These are my babies.
The clouds white as a wedding dress.

I stayed. You’d borrowed the light.
I wanted it back. I wore black.
You’d buy roses, still called it love
as I hid a bruise, another fracture.
The children cried and I
was too small to comfort their hurts.
The pain they wake to is not theirs.

I crushed pills, added water,
watched it turn colourless, tried to drink.
In the ambulance, my heart still beat
so healthily it almost bloomed.
This living doll was mended again
for the gift of my babies' small breaths,
the smell of their sleeps.

title quote from Sylvia Plath in interview

“Even amidst fierce flames the golden lotus can be planted”

Not the pink of a woollen wedding dress,
the azaleas on a cemetery path,
a bandage bloodied by a cut thumb,

nor the hearse-like English cars,
the men in crow-shaded suits
the shadow of Devonshire slate roofs.

Not the blues of the English Channel,
the Atlantic Ocean that tempted
drowning-dreams in her first decade.

Not Spanish terracotta or Devon earth.
Her red was the poppies’ papery skirts,
the lust for poetry in her blood.

Not quite the yellow of her bikini
during that platinum summer
of beaches and babysitting.

Almost the yellow of daffodils,
her first hive of bees (her father
had written *Bumblebees and their Ways*).

Her yellow was that of the rose -
Victorian symbol of jealousy,
rages that could tip her into self-loathing.

The yellow of a single rose bud
at the point of becoming a full bloom.

(title quote used on Sylvia Plath's headstone)

Manifesto
(*im Penelopeanne Dalgleish 1977 - 2002*)

Features in *Rugby World*, webzines and Safeways.
Your shock obituary - fatal accident.
The blood-jet stopped five years short of thirty.

Compare *The Rabbit Catcher*'s *like birth pangs*
with "today we argued. In your blackest mood
we saw the traps. You never understood England".

They'll still be desperate to print at 50.
You apprenticed at 25 to a profession
where suicide seemed a sensible career move.

Widely promote poetry to whom it belongs.
Readers: you're sophisicated, passionate,
playful. Prepare to be shaken from your groove.

Critics

Some read into the gaps between words:
as if inspecting the weave of the cloth,
the method of stitching, the quality of the fabrics.

They carefully unpick the garment,
spread it out to see its pattern
the parts from which it was sewn.

The critic stitches it back together
hanging it on a mannequin of the writer,
repeats with the next garment, and the next;

becomes more confident with each re-stitching,
begins to display the remade clothes,
but objects to others commenting

on a frayed buttonhole, an uneven hem,
two parts joined with incorrect stitching;
whether the garment still fits the writer.

Using French Knots for Bluebells

Complete all the two-strand stitches:
satin leaves, stems, ready for flower buds

Select the right shade of blue:
the positive pregnancy test is a good guide.

Pick a single strand, push needle through and hold,
like that moment between test and result,

wrap the thread around the needle at least three times.
A little knot of cells had latched to a womb's lining.

Ease the needle back through the cloth:
the knot should fix.

If not, the advice is to forget and try again
- think of it as a dropped stitch.

Embroidery keeps the hands busy.

Free Champagne in St Petersburg

In the lobby waiting for Amanda,
while avoiding eye contact with Finns
slurring their speech and making drinking motions,
I watch you pause to admire your manly reflection
in the metallic lift doors. Your back straightens,
hands go in pockets, stride lengthens,
expression eases into a half-smile.
A casual peacock in check shirt and jeans.

I wish I'd worn a longer skirt.
My spine curves back into the seat.
I resist glancing at my watch:
it wouldn't make Amanda apply lipstick any quicker.
I wonder if I could blink and make you disappear.
Or accompany the next Finn, intent on leaving
alcohol-restrictions at the border, to the bar.

You slide into the chair next to me
and offer a cigarette. Without noticing me not
take one, after establishing I speak English,
you tell me you're Dutch, disassociating
yourself from the surrounding poverty,
and holidaying alone. You have a yacht,
apparently, but fail to tell me what it looks like.
Or where it's moored. Or what it's named.

Breaking from your fascination with my skirt's pattern,
you ask if I would like a drink and make off
for the bar before I can shake my head.
I focus on the lift doors in your absence,
willing them to burst open with Amanda's lipsticked smile,
but the lobby echoes with silence.

A cheap champagne bottle and two glasses announce
your return. You pour and suggest moving somewhere private.
That I don't know your name is too feeble an excuse,
and not one that would concern you. I propose you
tell me your room number and go on up.
Then quietly raise my glass to your retreating back.
Now I know how to avoid you.

Sunlight: North Dublin

Squint-inducing sunlight
stops me here momentarily
looking up at a tenement block.
Damp babygros, teenagers' jeans
mums' skirts hang on improvised
washing lines on thin balconies.
Each floor sinks into the one below.
Each wall home to graffiti tags.
Rubbish stirs in the breeze.
The sunlight seems stronger
for being squeezed in the gap
between this block and a stark silhouette
of a city-grime encrusted church
putting these lives in shadow.

The Linden Hotel

Come and stay at The Linden Hotel
where you'll have a view of the lime trees
that obscure the graveyard of the Holy Trinity
and can watch wedding parties - bridesmaids
and bride carefully lifting her skirt and train -
as they walk to the park for photographs
that are not permitted on the Vicarage lawn.

Wander along Regent Street
and admire the double mini-roundabout.
Take a stroll to the Clock Tower
and watch the neon lights of the precinct.
For your evening's entertainment
there's Singles' Night at the Chasers nightclub,
divorcees' night at the Princes Bar
or the crib match at the British Legion.

As you leave
give the marbled steps of The Linden a quick polish.
You can erase all traces of having been there.

The sun's strength left with the holidaymakers

but this café remains open.
Most customers are known by name and chatter
about granddaughters (clever), grandsons (athletic)
or gaze at an empty seat whilst ordering
at patient waitresses with plump accents
who try not to notice how faded the silk flowers are.

Olivia

Congrats on the birth of Olivia
the card in the hairdresser's says.
But the daughter and friend
missing for 24 hours is today's only story.

At the end of Olivia's first day
a celebrity appeals
for the girls to phone they're OK.
No trace of their mobile signal.

The end of Olivia's first week:
fingertip searches, false leads,
tearful appeals
and a jogger reports earth mounds.

At the end of Olivia's first month:
The courts adjourn.
The media call grief-tourists morbid,
request families be left alone.

At the end of Olivia's first decade
she knows the drill: tell someone where you are,
phone home:
we're not checking up, we care.

At the back of Olivia's mother's mind, something nags.
A memory: something about a girl
a shared name,
a dead signal.

Jayne's Reflection

A plain Jayne the mirror said
until the fist-bruise-shadow
resisted her efforts at concealment
and edged into conversations
beyond the lee of mountain-obligation
sealed with a gold ring on her third finger.

Hearing the talk, she teased off her ring
and emerged from a cracked home
to let her bruises fade in the light.
She skated away on hesitant feet
as if a dance on clear ice,
whose steadying glass image called her Jayne.

Tiger

Emma called you Tiger:
a big name for a little cat.

Her case changed the definition of provocation
to include accumulated violence.

You blink away from the sunlight:
outside is bright with trial and error.

She had blinked in the prison exit's sunlight,
the brightness of her own flat.

Let's count your tabby stripes.
Say fifteen for kittenhood.

At fifteen she ran away
to Nottingham's inner city streets.

Let your sandpaper tongue wash
your dull metal-grey fur.

She used a knife on the pimp
about to rape her again.

Let's count two more stripes
as you stretch onto your long spine.

She was sentenced to seven years,
but served ten.

You've no problem with appetite.
Over three years you watched her diminish.

Count thirty stripes of your silver.

(from a photo accompanying Emma Humphrey's obituary)

Julie

Wore kitten-heeled boots
skin-tight jeans, studded belt
and a leather jacket,
feather-cut blonde hair
with heavy kohl and mascara
to age her blue eyes.

Huddles on a park bench
at midnight.
There's a gap in her pocket
where her stepmother refused
to give her house keys
and locked up an hour
before she said she would.

Dreams in snatches of sleep
a job at the perfume counter,
marriage to the guy she met tonight
because he once mentioned
he didn't want children.

Garden of Remembrance

She walks as if lost in thought
taking small steps in high-heeled sandals.
Her toe nails are painted pearly-pink.
Her manicured hands heavy with rings.
She wears a thin belt at her waist.
Her red handbag hangs across her body.
Her hair, brushed so the brown covers grey,
is pulled into a net and secured by a clip.
Rouge traces the hollow of her cheekbones.
Kohl and mascara add a little expression
to a face softened by anti-wrinkle cream.
She chooses to sit away from the flowerbeds.
Her eyes check that she has been seen.
She is accustomed to being thought beautiful.

Human Resources Advisor

She twists the ruby ring on her middle finger,
speaks in phrases from an official script.

She's had her mouse brown hair highlighted,
is here to tell me my job is at risk.

The company car seatbelt crumpled her blouse.
"Is there another job in the company you have the skills to do?"

Fuck off and read my personnel file:
I'm not helping you to make me redundant.

Her matching skirt and jacket is a tweed-effect in pink and green:
the calming colours the DSS paints its waiting rooms.

Snapshot

Scalds have blanched dark skin.
Her nose ends in a large scab.
Scars, the size and shape of a cigarette tip,
litter her skin like acne.
Her mouth is parted, knowing
it should smile for the camera.

Her infant's eyes look for a friend
who could tell her story.
She is months away from death.
Someone recorded, reported
and passed the file, like a child
dodging pass-the-parcel's forfeit.

Echoes

Uphill, upstairs, first landing,
first self-contained flat:
Victorian Gothic windows on Gotham Street.
Freedom from complaints about my music,
common in a shared house.
I left echoes of your favourite song
and his photo of you on a barstool smiling
days before your murder.
I light a scented candle,
scribble a new poem.

Retreat

There was no big bang
just a series of small ones
in his morning kitchen clattering and curses
that moved the cats to retreat.

Two pairs of green eyes watched her
close the door between them.
Before providing comfort
she stabbed at the stereo's buttons
for the radio to give
a sheen of anti-listening.

Shiver

Sax notes drift from the subway
to a bone-delicate sky
shadowed by the high rise blocks
and for a moment
morning city sounds fade
to a midnight hour,
feet feel warped beer-sticky boards,
band swamped by cigarette fog
and a crowded venue's humidity,
a sequinned singer spotlighted
with a voice to unite
and a warm that could unfreeze my cold hands
and melt this winter day
as sax notes shiver my spine.

Testing

One: his lonely note
echoes in an empty venue,
no audience
to reverberate against.

Two: she's there
in the middle of the crowd.
Blonde/ brunette
cosmetically perfect
sexy in a clingy dress.

Testing: the boundaries
of her space,
the taste of her lips,
smoothness of her skin,
her point of give.

One, two: more confident now:
me, you.

We're told we don't deserve you

On-stage in a sleeveless tee shirt
deliberately baggy to reveal
a gym-worked torso.

Leather jeans, black,
to make those thin
legs appear longer.

Skin so white, so gothically
pale as it twists
in mirror-practised moves.

Chiselled cheekbones
helped with a hint
of blusher.

Eyebrows shaved
and then pencilled in
so the arch is just right.

Strike your Jesus pose,
the mic stand your cross.
Make us believe.

Make us feel
the adrenalin rush
of song-choked emotion.

As the rhythm demands dance,
give us the chill
of true entertainment.

Don't merely sell us the CD,
ensure it reverberates
in a weeks'-long ringing in our ears.

Leave us
with an aching void
like amphetamine comedown.

But,
amongst feedback and empty stage,
your song-parables just don't cut it.

“When I open my mouth to sing, I’m bigger”

because:

I wasn’t a kinderwhore/ dollpart
didn’t have a girlish name
didn’t pierce my labia, call it art,

because:

I was always part of the band
round my hips slung a real guitar
played riffs that musos couldn’t imitate
tucked short blonde hair behind one ear.
I stood tall before the mic stand.

They photoed my callused hands
labelled me grandmother.

Title is a quote from Kim Gordon (of rock bands Sonic Youth, Harry Crews and Free Kitten)

The Lightship

Music thumps from the party-hired Lightship
drowning out laughter and dancing.

Out here the cobblestones are uneven and cracked,
difficult for stiletto heels.

Paint flakes off bent bars of metal fencing.
The Lightship's beacon flickers idly.

The city sounds distant.
The hour before pubs close and night clubs open

Tarnished lights appear n midnight water
briefly appear as fake diamonds on inky velvet.

I tore up your letters. The ebb took the fragments
out to sea: to lose them in its expanse.

Blink.
Scum, debris scuff the harbour wall.

Loved

Through a window square
bereaved of light
the day turns ghost.

Fabric creates a barrier.
Candlelight adds ambience.
Scattered rose petals on the floor.

Guitar-string flattened fingers
caress the piano,
dark nails against white keys.

Alice in her party dress-
ed to kill.

Break for a nicotine fix.
Her lipstick ring on a cigarette
provokes a lyric.

Her presence lingers,
as the cigarette burns to ash.
The song tastes of frost.

After the Gig

I - The Fan

He stands,
charcoal grey pinstriped suit
still immaculate
although the white shirt cuffs
are now grubby,
amongst feedback and roadies;
isolated in imposed idleness.
Long, bony fingers
push jet black hair
from his mask-like face,
not sure what to do
without microphone or beer.
Thin mouth, after singing,
relaxes into something
approximating a smile.
His dark eyes watch.

Not security or a roadie,
yet you're a barrier.
Your black lyrca dress
presses your stomach flat.
You cloud in perfume.
Your foundation was polyfilla'd:
there's too much kohl,
not enough mascara.
Your eyes are just
a little too bright,
as you talk to no one,
least of all the man
you're describing as genius.

I slide past and ask him
how he got that producer.
Offer him a drink
that he gratefully accepts.
His words tumble
in enthusiasm,
his Californian accent
more pronounced,
his smile more genuine.
You glare.
But a beer's more
refreshing than sycophancy.
He grins his thanks.

After the Gig

II - The Ligger

Oh, I am just so drained!
My voice has almost gone
but when he did my favorite...
Oh, the intelligence of his lyrics!
His songs are just genius.

What the...?

I hate her already:
she just slipped between those cases!

Who is she?
She's short -
only comes up to his buttonhole
despite those heels.
Flat too: no curves on her.
She's gotta be a six.
Bet she needs that jacket to keep warm.
Her hair's limp and mousey.
Can't smell perfume:
she probably uses soap.
And is that shadow
or smudged kohl?
Has that lipstick bled?

How dare she!
She's not worthy.

A beer!
Gotta be the wrong brew.
What would she know?

He's smiling.
What are they *talking* about?

After the Gig

III - The Singer/ Songwriter

It's over.
Didn't seem too bad.
Sound was lousy:
PA was ancient.
But the crowd made it:
really good atmosphere.

Now what?
I guess I stand here.
Outta the way.
Let the roadies get on with it.
I've done my fair share of humping.

She's off again.
The one with the earrings
as golden as that Californian tan
under the white theatre paint.
I've forgotten her name, again.
Forgotten even how she came to be here.

I'm not a genius: I'm a singer.
I'm not a poet: I write lyrics.
And right now I'd like a beer.

Now, she's genuinely pale
against that black fishnet.
There're nerves beneath that smile.
Her accent's British, polite,
as she asks about my songs.
There's a story behind that producer...
And thanks for the beer.

Go on, glare from under that white paint.
Her questions interest unlike your statements.
Yeah, I'm missing my wife,
but I'm wearing my wedding band
and you don't have one, but might as well have.

Yellow Torchlight and the Blues

Inside Saturday night shines dull
on yellowed walls
through beer-fumed tobacco-fog.

Cramped in a corner
the drummer's invisible
but the beat's real
driving below
the pit of conversation.
Musicians appear as blind watchers
sensing their way through songs
viperous eyes all but closed.

She's torchlit blonde
in a slimming widow-black.
Blue eyeshadow creeps into folds
it was carefully brushed over.
Lipstick bleeds into fine lines.
Only the sax would know her age.

Her cigarette-scarred voice
packs emotion into facile rhymes
as she sings
achingly
alone.

Suddenly time's gained an hour
she's faded from view
the bar shuts
walls sweat condensation.

Outside autumn lights a flare
and through the empty backstreets
The Floating Harbor
ripples blue accompaniments
to Billie Holiday's *Gloomy Sunday*.

Absence

(im Rozz Williams (1964 - 1998)
singer, writer of "HEROnlysIN" who took his own life)

The floor, pockmarked by stilleto heels,
has a grey dust cover:
trails of your bleak childmemories.

The air is no longer weighted
by lyrics and sound waves pounding from a PA...

...your songs dense-layered as Jupiter,
fierce as launch rockets:
HEROnlysIN: the "yeah, I'll try"
that tamed depression
that became a craving.

In this venue painted as black as your shirt
- always long-sleeved -
my feet shuffle a remembered rhythm
and I spin in the absence of a crowd.

Your eyes dark against a starwhite skin
concealer over lackofsleep eyebruises.

The mic stand's a conqueror's flag pole.
You claimed your own life.

Interview with the Popstar

The popstar
takes a polaroid of the Interviewer
against a cloudless sky.

America is shown in movie widescreen:
barren landscapes in which to search for a soul,
Talk turns to the cut-up lyric technique:

the Interviewer explains: take an article
(another's), cut into phrases, rearrange into song-shapes
and leave meaning to materialise

or to be invented by journalists.
During the Interviewer's chatter, word count highest scores
go to *chameleon* and *changes*.

Under the creeping moonlight,
to a relaxed Popstar whose closed mouth smiles
the Interviewer still talks.

Courtney Love's First Interview after becoming a Widow

Another hotel room.
Another interview.
Another cigarette.

From under rumpled peroxide hair vacant green eyes
indicate the valium has not yet worn off.

You freely admit he called you that night,
but recording your music was more important.
You say you couldn't cope with him.
You thought you'd cleared the house of guns.

The Prozac kicks in. You get up,
floating to an imagined rhythm.
Ever seen a cripple dance?
you complain no one pays attention to your music.
Your scars are non-permanent bruises.

You gave us a re-released "Doll Parts" single.

And, perhaps after your out-pourings,
we don't need the music.

Please stop telling me how good the Velvet Underground were

An obituary marches
forward to page three.
Can't miss this one,
trailered on the front pages, just in case.
A body deprived of drugs
took life from your hero,
leaving you frightened in the still hours.
Almost scared to play the records, the videos:
the dead ought not be seen to be alive.
Might as well do the mortgage
the pension thing now
and resign yourself to morn
with gestures as large as the headlines.

My heroes are on the pub circuit
or large in Europe.
They've never even had a one line
throwaway, filler review,
The record shop assistant still says, "Who?"
even after being given
catalogue reference and barcode.
Death is defined as fading into obscurity
or joining the *stupid club*
and goes unobiturariéd.
Until weeks-late articles
claiming to have known all along:
so why didn't they publish?

A Life in 14 Moves

1

The pregnancy test was blue confirmation.
That cliché: swept off her feet in a whirlwind
and charmed into being emotionally blind.
She could not contemplate an abortion,
knew she could cope: already was a single mother
(doubts crept in about his fathering ability -
drug misuse? - mood swings and inconsistency).
A daughter was happy to welcome a brother.
A long labour - over twenty-four hours
a baby wanting to explore, to move towards light
yet aware he was leaving the womb's comfort
for a mother's relief in a room showered with flowers.
His bright alertness was to become more than it seems
was it razor-edged punk rebellion dreams?

2

Was it razor-edged, thrash punk rebellion dreams
or awareness of being the only male in a female household
that encouraged a toddler to see French as cold
but Spanish worth learning? Dividing the house into teams:
"stupid language", "good language", "I'll speak as I want".
Precociousness was welcomed: mother desired a bright child,
a wish for him to inherit a book-loving world,
to nurture talent, give him an intellectual start.
But could a child be too bright?
Could he be lapping up his teachers' attention,
using wit and charm as a deflection
from an underlying problem, some blight
that only his mother suspected was there:
a long lament that span down beyond despair?

3

A long lament that span down beyond despair:
two children, a busy, self-employed mother,
yet there was another romance, a potential step-father:
this one with staying power, an aptitude for care
and a love for children, even if not his own.
Wedding bells rang, adoption forms signed,
the family began to expand
and oldest brother played the clown.
Became a teenager interested in self-expression.
Saw a friend fatally injured in a car accident.
Then stayed all day in bed, mourning wouldn't relent.
Busy, mother wouldn't give concessions.
Those duvet days, apparent lack of care
expressed a bleak enclosure of paranoid fear.

4

Expressed a bleak enclosure of paranoid fear
by writing songs, sang to strummed guitar chords -
saw himself on stage in front of screaming hordes
of fans, recipient of letters stained with tears,
king of a hundred and one chat shows,
lifestyle guru, policy advisor, campaigner
with a host of staff on generous retainers
to forecast, implement and ideally kow-tow
to his ideas. More modest were the fantasises
told to impress women into holiday romances,
to turn impressionable peers into lackeys,
discarded like loose coins in a foreign currency.
Should he write romantically-stringed songs of dreams
or songs with impulsive pounding rhythms.

5

Or songs with impulsive, pounding rhythms:
music to live by or to hide within.
He was supposed to be understanding:
a favourite sister was getting married, seems
the whole family's happy. Except part of him
feels bereft, as if losing a best friend,
a relationship's come to an end
and no one had bothered to consult him.
Told to be on his very best behaviour,
he turned up late, in torn jeans and a smile
insisted on giving a speech while
his mother squirmed. To the guests he was a saviour
from stuffy formality. They toasted him to the sky.
Could he have an audience to be loved by?

6

Could he have an audience to be loved by?
He formed a band: schoolfriends who could play
and were prepared to rehearse every day
they could. Never asked him or wondered why
his mother put pressure on him to conform,
to behave like his siblings, to be polite in company,
diligently to do schoolwork, eat with the family,
compress himself into her idea of norm.
With the band he could take command,
dictate lyrics, chord structures, tempo,
song list order, whether to play the show,
could inspire an audience with the wave of a hand,
temporarily be a leader amongst men:
a mindscape that could encompass all these moods and then...

7

A mindscape that could encompass all these moods and then
some: the sheer joy of the lightness of being
suddenly becoming a deep hole of mourning
or an amazing, generous sweep of passion,
with a strength and conviction that no one
could resist: powerful enough to the melt the stone-
hearted, inflame short term thinkers with vision.
But a mother warned he wasn't like his peers.
Step-father scanned books, searched the internet,
listed and compared symptoms, couldn't find an alike set.
Doctors were consulted, lists of suitable counsellors
drawn up to deal with a teenager's brooding, sullen
moods, some changing slowly, lasting for minutes or a sudden

8

Some changing slowly, lasting for minutes or a sudden
flip, as if in binary logic: zero or one.
Rarely smoothed by analogue's sine wave. On
a chance consultation, at the age of sixteen,
he was labelled: a-typical manic depression.
Finally. The label brought relief
confirming a mother's long-held belief
her bright son was different, now she had confirmation.
But she couldn't relax: something could be done.
There could be counselling, medication.
Case studies summarised into a distillation
of facts. While losing sight of the son
as a loving, individual, guitar-playing guy:
while on stage he could pretend to be ordinary.

9

While on stage he could pretend to be ordinary.
Mother's pressure ensured he was given a prescription
for lithium, despite the consultant's explanation
of side effects including damage to kidneys,
the need to constantly monitor the dosage
- lithium can be toxic - to be as low as possible
while still being effective. Some find it desirable
to retain some mood changes. His age
made it difficult to diagnose with any confidence.
As well as a counsellor, he gained two minders.
After an attempted overdose, they became his keepers:
following him almost everywhere with diligence
and discretion. On stage with other performers
he was away from prescribed drugs, counsellors, minders.

10

Away from prescribed drugs, counsellors, minders
out in a world of his own making. In front
of an audience, an appreciative crowd, a slant
from the real world wanted by his mother.
A previous band was told of his condition:
his mother insisted on honesty but didn't tell
him they knew and made it sound like hell.
Suddenly they could only see the label, not him.
He warned: the new band was not to be told.
This band had to stay together: his right
to free expression, to have a spotlight
for his talent, not to end up cold-
shouldered as he had previously,
no threats to his right to medical privacy.

11

No threats to his right to medical privacy
no one else should know of the "dragon within"
(as his mother called it). As if he could split: him
and the dragon, leaving spare capacity -
for what? Exquisite manners? Could he live without it?
Or was it as much part of him as songwriting?
Was separation desirable? Or would the splitting
leave him less confidence plus doubts?
The dragon gave him his creativity,
his strength and humour, his abilities, his charm,
his intelligence, his speed, his enthusiasm,
his lateral intuition, his generosity.
Was it right to view him so negatively,
rid him of the "dragon within" that was his personality?

12

Rid him of the “dragon within” that was his personality?
Watch him perform out there on stage
with a mental agility beyond his age,
why should he be viewed only negatively?
Was it genuine concern or a worry he wasn’t “normal”?
Remember his funny stories, his ease
with a crowd, eagerness to please.
OK, so he misbehaved at formal
events, wasn’t as easy as his siblings,
couldn’t set his own boundary
although he always tried
to curb his excesses without clipping
his wings. Despite the counsellors
even good performances were stress triggers.

13

Even good performances were stress triggers.
Successful shows could be brilliant in one mood, in
another a loved song could become a terrible din,
the show a feat of endurance: a crowd of sniggers,
lazy technicans, over-zealous management,
an unfulfilled rider, band members lousy players,
equipment inadequate, stage cramped... until layers
of frustration build: everyone becomes incompetent.
Suddenly the audience want an encore,
demand a favourite song
and out comes a performance worthy of a gong
(Grammy or Best International Newcomer) to scare
off the competition, until the mood abates.
He knew there was as many loves as there were hates.

14

He knew there were as many loves as there were hates,
knew nothing could be done the same way twice,
knew he was paying the price
as the moods took their toll. Chose a meaningless date,
took an overdose of morphine, found himself hospitalised.
Was advised he'd have an anaphylactic reaction
(a small dose of morphine could kill). Compassion
and love he received from siblings. His mother was scandalised,
employed two minders so he could be looked after 24/7.
No time was his own. Until, one tour,
he found a window around 4 am - only an hour -
but long enough for him to gamble on a decision
after an excellent show, on a high without hate
he loaded the syringe with morphine: dared the fates.

15

He loaded the syringe with morphine: dared the fates,
knew there were as many loves as there were hates.
Even good performances were stress triggers,
couldn't rid him of the "dragon within" that was his personality
or threats to break his right to medical privacy.
Away from prescribed drugs, counsellors, minders...
out on stage where he could pretend to be ordinary
changing slowly or lasting for minutes or a sudden
flip. A mindscape that could encompass all these moods and then
some. As vocalist did he have an audience to be loved by?
Songs with impulsive, pounding rhythms
expressing a bleak enclosure of paranoid fear
or a long lament that span down beyond despair
or was it razor-edged, thrash punk rebellion dreams?

Autumn Colours

A small red car stands undisturbed
in a railway station car park.

    A low sunrise reflection on a signal
    can make red appear yellow.

    Diesel may burn at nearly 1000°C:
    hotter than a crematorium furnace.

The red car has been there since six am
on a fine autumn Tuesday.

    A chorus of mobile phones were left ringing
    or diverted to a computerised message service.

    First aid kits taken from sales shelves
    were not regarded as lost profit.

Its number plate whitened on days of frosts;
the red car remains untouched.

Leicester to Planet X

A sudden stop at Chesterfield
wheels on rails screech feedback:
a sound technican's signal failed
amongst angered guitars,
must make Liverpool by 20:30.

Time warps like a retro band,
who think the seventies are *really* now:
two hours feels like four
A slow silence murmurs
- strings sampled out of context -
builds a buzzing crescendo of irritation.
Headliners start at ten.

It's now eight and with no rehearsal
the train jerks into the motion
of a bassist a bar behind the drummer.

A station screen flickers cancellation
with the pulsed insistency of a strobe.
Solid as a bouncer, the stationmaster tells me
I'm stranded at Sheffield Pond Street.

Rain beats onto the platform:
I resent the way it sounds
like stamped demands for an encore
to a stage empty but for a drained glass
and an abandoned plectrum.

Painting the Bedroom
(*for Paul*)

Fresh airdraughts are cold contrast
to your body's warm welcome.

Teasing bristles into corners.
Our kisses in anticipation.

Paintbrush along slender sill.
My tongue, your spinelength.

Gloss caressing stripped wood.
My lips, your flat stomach.

Brushstrokes fall into rhythm.
Your surfaces cover mine.

My catchbreath sigh: last touch.
Your pleasure at the result.

Miranda's Warning

Hey Mum, you've the right to remain silent
about the time you (quietly) threatened to put me on the shelf
when I wanted the pram's motion to rock me to sleep
and you wanted to stop and actually pay for groceries.

Anything you say can and will be used against you
in my "so famous I only need my first name
despite my unsupportive, inadequate mother"
theme in my future bestselling autobiography.

You may have a nutritional expert present
when I blame my eating disorder and body dysmorphia
on your rewarding me with pacifying chocolate
instead of encouraging me to eat my greens.

If you cannot afford a lawyer -
having funded my pocket money and your Mother's Day bouquets -
when I sue you for genetic proof you're my parent:
that's just tough.

You know, Mum, anytime you wish,
you can decide to stay silent and not answer any questions.
Could you consider this really, really carefully,
especially at Parents' Evenings.

Bearing the above in mind, do you still want to talk to me, Mum?
Mum?